Beer

Udo Pini

Beer

Feierabend

Cont

© 2003 Feierabend Verlag oHG

Mommsenstraße 43, D-10629 Berlin, Germany

Project coordination: Bettina Freeman

Translation from German: Heather Stacey, Edinburgh

Editing: Lizzie Gilbert, Cologne

Typesetting: Roman Bold & Black, Cologne

Concept and coordination: Redaktionsbüro Udo Pini, Hamburg

Picture desk: Nicola Kossel

Design: Lutz Jahrmarkt, Drage

Lithography: kölnermedienfabrik, Cologne

Printing and binding: poligrafici calderara spa

Printed in Italy

ISBN 3-936761-56-6

61-04013-1

ents

Good health!

Even looking down on them, these beers are no longer simply proletarian thirst quenchers. They are now specialties that confront us with choices: thirst, whim, curiosity, or just the pleasure of beer?

Beer is over 6,000 years old, as will be seen. And yet it remains fresh and sparkling and is constantly being reinvented. It should not just be celebrated as a great **triumph** of humankind over unpredictable wild yeasts, but also acknowledged as a cultural phenomenon and great conversational companion. Beer is as good-natured as most of its fans, whose **strength of character** makes up for the drink's low alcohol content. The fact that there are beers that are luxury drinks or so strong as to render people literally speechless are exceptions which are sought out by **connoisseurs** and arouse the curiosity of a younger generation, for whom a whole new world of specialty beers is being created. Because every beer drinker selects the beer that suits them best!

Beer is...

Kingly connoisseur
In 1995 Sweden's King Carl Gustaf and Queen Silvia visited the Czech Budweiser Budvar Brewery and sipped the traditional drink politely as others down it with gusto

The people's thirst
A liter/quart glass is the best remedy for a real beer thirst, a long draught from the bottle quenches thirst the quickest, and a beer-to-go in a plastic cup from a pub can also be enjoyed after closing time. If you ever drink a glass of beer too quickly, like former German chancellor, Helmut Kohl, you can contemplate whether the glass is half empty or still half full

People

and beer

You can enjoy a sip, fancy a tipple, have a quick one, **down a few,** knock it back, send it down the hatch, try it as a child and later never pass it up – beer has been a part of life for centuries and has even gained a **premium image** as a global drink.

bira
Interlingua

bil
Volapük

biro
in Ido

⠃⠊⠑⠗
Braille

biero
in Esperanto

ab'jo
in Iran (Farsi)

alus
in Latvia
and Lithuania

beer/ale
in Britain

beera
in Israel

**beereh
(birae)**
in Arabic

beoir
in Ireland (Gaelic)

bere
in Romania

bia
in Thailand
and Vietnam

bia/pombe
in Swahili

Bier
in Germany,
Austria, parts
of Switzerland

bier
in the Netherlands
and South Africa
(Afrikaans)

bière
in France

biiru
in Japan

bir
in Indonesia,
Malaysia, and
in Yiddish

bira
in Bulgaria

"Beer
international

Cheers!
When Europe
shipped "export
beer" all over
the world it
was welcomed
everywhere
and from then
on competed
with the words
for local beers

bira
in Turkey

bîre
in Kurdish

birra
in Italy

birrë
in Albania

biyar/jad
in Nepal

cerevisia, cervisia
in Latin and
Vatican City

cerveja
in Portugal

cerveza
in Spanish worldwide

cerveja/ cervexa
in Galician

garagardoa
in Basque

cervesa
in Catalan

cwrw
in Wales

in Gestuno

jij
in Chechnya

leann, lionn, beòir
in Scotland
(Scottish Gaelic)

mek-ju
in Korea

mpira, tzythos
in Greece

öl
in Sweden

øl
in Denmark and
Norway

öl, bjór
in Iceland

õlu
in Estonia

olut, kalja
in Finland

pi jiu
in China (Mandarin)

pia
in Hawaii

piva
in Belarus

pivo
in Russia,
Serbia,
the Slovak Republic,
Ukrainia, Slovenia,
Azerbaijan,
Croatia, and the
Czech Republic

piwo
in Poland

serbesa
in Tagalog
(Philippines)

sör
in Hungary

utshwala
in Zulu

vuola
in Lapland
(in Sami)

A world of words for beer

Whenever wild yeast and sugar came together the end result was beer – all over the world. In Early Sumerian, fermentable "beer bread" was called "bapir", the beverage itself was "kash", which survived among the Slavs as fermented "kvas", while the Akkadian word, "bapiru" was shortened to "piro" and from there probably became the Eastern European "pivo". The etymology of the word used in Central Europe ("beer/Bier/bière/birra") is unclear, possibly it is derived from the monastic Latin word "biber" (drink). Or perhaps it comes from a Germanic word "beuza" (to froth) – from which it might follow that "bhr-" and "bher-" were the roots of the words for brewing. From the Germanic "alut" (bitter) for un-hopped beer come the English word "ale" and the Nordic "öl/øl". The fourth word for beer in Europe established itself in the Romance languages from the Latin/Celtic "cervisia", after Ceres, goddess of agriculture and grain, giving us the Spanish "cerveza".

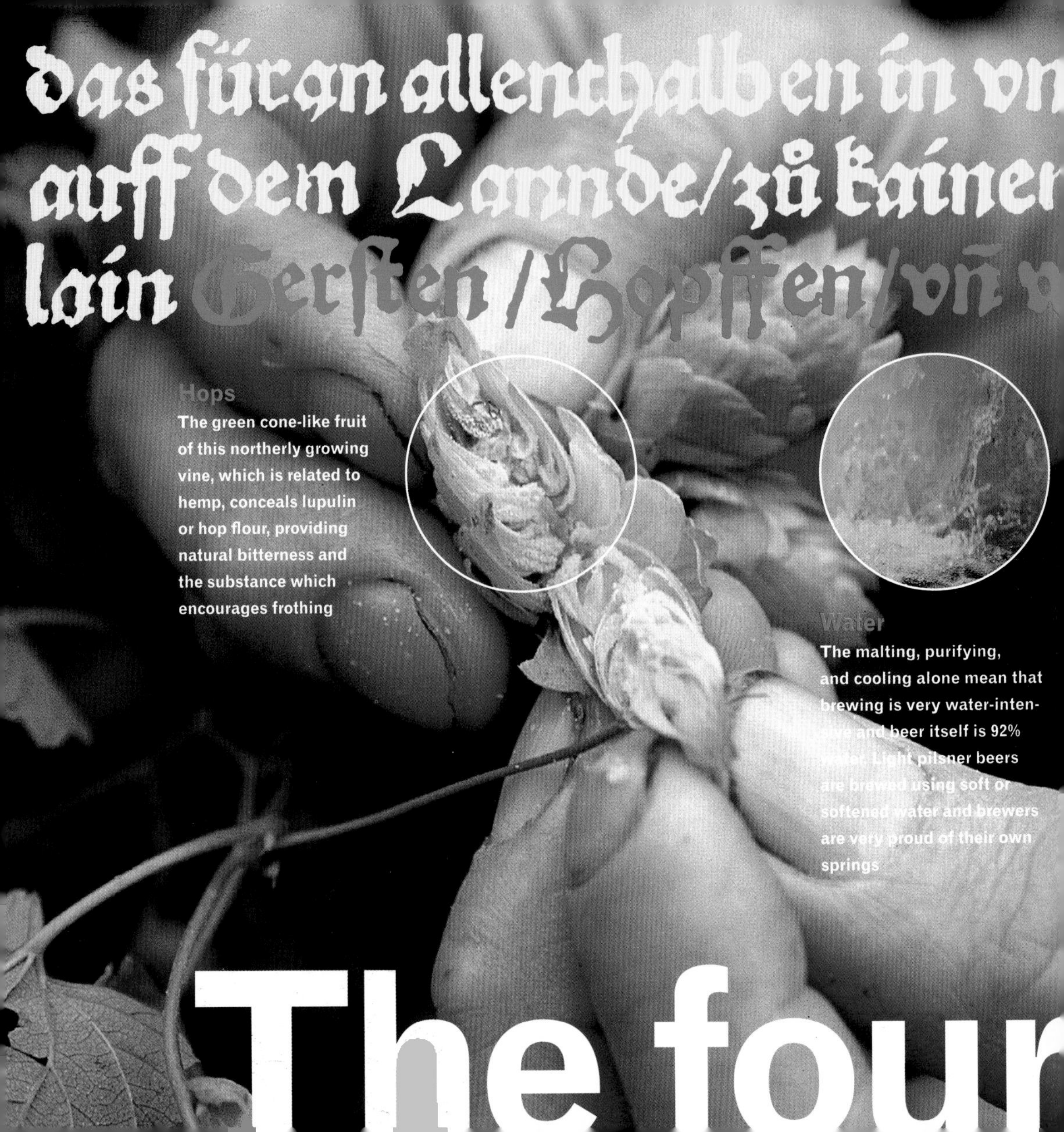

das für an allenthalben in vn
auff dem Lannde/zů kainer
lain Gersten/Hopffen/vn̄ v

Hops

The green cone-like fruit
of this northerly growing
vine, which is related to
hemp, conceals lupulin
or hop flour, providing
natural bitterness and
the substance which
encourages frothing

Water

The malting, purifying,
and cooling alone mean that
brewing is very water-inten-
sive and beer itself is 92%
water. Light pilsner beers
are brewed using soft or
softened water and brewers
are very proud of their own
springs

The four

ern Stetten/Märcktehen/vñ
Pier/ merer stück / dañ al-
sser/genomen vñ gepraucht

Malted barley

All grains can be used for brewing beer but barley is best. Germination is initiated to produce "green malt". Once optimum enzyme levels are reached, further germination is prevented by kiln drying. The longer and hotter the drying process, the darker the malt and the color of the beer

Brewer's yeast

After grinding, steeping, and heating the malt (mash), the yeast breaks down the sugar in the resulting "wort" into alcohol and carbon dioxide. "Bottom-fermenting" yeast sinks to the bottom, "top-fermenting" yeast rises foaming to the top

Had Europe's brewers not discovered **hops** in the 16th century, we would still be drinking awful beers with all sorts of flavor enhancers. The attractive cone-like female flowers of the native hop vine produce a bitter but aromatic substance which acts as a preservative in beer and also helps to make it froth. Brewing is now an ultra clean industrial process using special yeast strains and so naturally occurring yeasts no longer generate or ruin beer by accident. In Germany the **Purity Law (Reinheitsgebot),** in force from 1516 but now optional, still preserves the beer's reputation, stipulating just four ingredients…

essentials

Bass

Ice crystals in British pale ale glow brilliantly in the polarized light of a Florida State University beer researcher's photomicroscope

Beauty in a micros

Beck's

These super thin ice crystals in Bremen's famous beer are about to melt and double refraction in polarized light shows up the fine, microscopic features of this beer brewed according to the German Purity Law

copic drop of beer

Pilsener Urquell
The first light, bottom-fermented beer in the world exhibits an almost three-dimensional quality in the structure around the center of the crystals in the thin frozen layer

Samuel Adams Triple Bock
This strong beer from Boston, USA, was matured in an oak barrel for four years and displays a dramatic optical power in its ice crystal structure

World champion drinkers

Countries are proud of many things, holding national records and ambitiously breaking them. However, in "Beer-drinking per head" the frontrunners seem to be unbeatable. The **Czechs,** who after all invented pilsner in 1842, are the world champions. The **Irish,** who gave us the "black stuff" (Guinness), are second.

The Germans, inventors of popular beers, such as bock beer, and hosts of major beer events, only come third. The **Northern Europeans** and Americans favor beer, while southern countries prefer wine but are making up ground. However, it's sizzling Australia which has long been a keen competitor for the title.

Hard to swallow
For a long time German national pride was boosted by being among the world's top beer drinkers but beer consumption is now decreasing world-wide and the Germans are no longer world champion beer guzzlers – they've been overtaken by the Czechs and the Irish

Sweden 56.4

Switzerland 57.8

South Africa 58.7

Cyprus 59.4

Poland 59.6

Hungary 61.6

Portugal 65.3

Canada 69.9

Spain 71.8

Venezuela 75.7

Finland 78.4

New Zealand 80.0

Foreign beer tastes better
National beer loyalty is not prevalent in Europe

Denmark
loves British beer

Germany
likes Danish beer

Spain
goes Dutch

France
likes Belgian beer

Ireland actually
drinks English

Italy loves
German beer

Luxembourg likes
Belgian beers

Austria
likes German beer

Portugal likes to
drink German

Finland
is fond of Irish

Sweden
likes Danish beer

United Kingdom
loves Irish beer

Norway likes
Swedish beer

Switzerland
drinks German

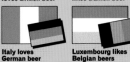

Netherlands 82.5

USA 84.1

Slovak Republic 87.5

Australia 95.0

United Kingdom 95.4

Belgium 98.2

Denmark 99.7

Luxembourg 107.9

Austria 108.1

Germany 125.5

Ireland 152.9

Czech Republic 160.0

Malting

It is the secret of partially germinating specially selected barley, halting germination at the right moment with heat (kilning), and the temperature used which determine the eventual flavor and color of the beer

Mashing

The ground malt is steeped in hot water to form a mixture called the mash; this is heated in batches and the starch is converted into sugar

Brewing

The sugary mash is then boiled, usually in copper brew kettles, hops or other flavorings are added, the mixture is cooled, cleared, and the resulting wort is transferred to the fermenting vat where the sugar provides nourishment to the yeast

Fermenting

Depending on the original gravity, pure brewer's yeasts convert sugar into more or less alcohol and carbon dioxide. Top and bottom-fermentation and beer types depend on the brewing temperature and yeast used

Brewing

"Too much water, not enough hops, beers like that put God in a strop!" Popular sentiment has always been vociferous about bad beer and once even led to **beer revolts.** In addition to experience and craftsmanship, brewing is now a rather exact science with standardized, industrially produced ingredients, plenty of **high-tech** equipment, and a few tricks. Brewmasters and product managers are strategists, always inventing new varieties to add to the established ones. Beer is brewed systematically for **target groups** and expansion is key. The brewing itself can be impaired by globalized competition and there have already been complaints of flavors becoming blander to appeal to the mass market. However, in spite of all the technical aids available, brewing is still a **craft** rich in tradition. The best beers remain a sensory triumph dependent on the nose of the master brewer.

Small is beautiful:

With an audience
In Freiburg's small Feierling
Brewery in southern
Germany visitors enjoy the
end product while the
brewmaster is busy at
the brew kettle preparing
the next batch

At first people laughed at these mini breweries with their adjoining bars, but since 1981 respect has grown in the USA for microbreweries and their **specialties.** Because they were small and keenly dedicated to quality, their master brewers became known by the honorary title of **craft brewers.** Initially, market jealousies confined them to small-scale production but they are now unrestricted. In addition, the **brewpubs** no longer have to serve half the beer they produce on site and sell the rest at high prices. Everything has been liberalized because microbreweries brew top-class beers. In Portland, USA, there are so many of them, the city is known as **"Munich on the Willamette"**.

microbreweries

With creativity

The master brewers are kings in the smaller breweries and they develop colorful specialty beers from stout to pale ale for their own bars

With high-tech equipment

The microbreweries are equal in every way to their larger rivals when it comes to equipment. The term "microbrewery" originated in the USA in 1981

Coca-Cola showed the way and the major breweries believe they can follow suit – conquering the world, ideally with one single brand, sold in barrels, bottles, and cans. The global beer empire mergers are becoming increasingly impenetrable but experienced tourists have long known which beers are available where. Regional brewers promote their specialties in response to the ease of the mass producers. In fact, like the giants, they just want to have the whole world on tap.

Global beers

6,000 yea

around 4000 BC beer brewing is depicted for the first time on Sumerian clay tablets **circa 3400 BC** the oldest image of beer drinkers appears on a clay vase in Iraq **around 3000 BC,** the Epic of Gilgamesh took form, where primitive man, Enkidu, only truly becomes human after consuming beer and bread **around 1700 BC** brewing and serving beer is chiefly women's work and daily beer rations are regulated in the cuneiform script of the Code of Hammurabi (workers 2 liters/quarts, civil servants 3 liters/quarts, administrators and high priests 5 liters/quarts) **around 1600 BC** an ancient Egyptian brewery is described on a clay tablet (the hieroglyph for meal is "beer + bread"), dates, aniseed, saffron, and honey are added to sweeten the brew **in 353 AD** an amphora of Roman beer disappears beneath the rubble of a fort near Mainz, to be found 1,600 years later and put in a museum **764** is the year of the earliest recorded German hop cultivation

815 sees the first reference to Munich beer **in 1040** the Weihenstephan brewery near Munich is founded, one of the oldest in the world still producing beer today **in 1294** King Gambrinus, alias Jan Primus, Duke of Brabant, unstoppable beer drinker, minnesinger, and womanizer, dies in a beer wager **in 1351** a "bockig" (stubborn) strong beer is brewed in Einbeck **in 1516** the Purity Law comes into force in Bavaria and from 1906 throughout Germany (until 1987, after which it is optional) **in 1589** the Munich Hofbräuhaus court brewery is founded (serving beer to the public from 1828) **in 1592** European beer is exported for the first time from France to North America **in 1605** the first wheat beer is brewed in Munich **1680** sees the first mention of Berlin wheat beer **in 1759** Arthur Guinness founds his porter brewery **in 1785** British inventor Joseph Bramah patents the beer-pump handle **1810** is the year of the first Munich Oktoberfest held on the meadow now known

rs of beer

as Theresienwiese **in 1842** the first pilsner-style beer is served in Pilsen **in 1873** Linde's new refrigeration machine means bottom-fermented lager beer can be stored ("lager" comes from German for store) and brewed all year round **in 1876** E. Anheuser and Co. launch their US Budweiser **1880** is the year when the largest number of commercial brew-eries were operating world-wide **in 1888** Foster's Beer appears on the American market **1892** sees a US patent for a new capping machine (100 bottles per minute); the invention of crown caps, beer mats, and the first glass liter/quart beer mugs; and the first "Wies'n Bier" is brewed, a strong but pale double bock **1920** marks the beginning of 13 years of Prohibition in the USA **in 1922** Bavarian landlord Franz Xaver Kugler almost runs out of beer, he dilutes it with lemonade and "Radler" (shandy) is invented **1933** sees the end of the "noble experiment" of Prohibition; 22 states and 100 counties remain "dry" **in 1935** the world's first beer can contains Krüger's Finest from Newton/NJ, but you still need a can opener **in 1963** US beer cans get removable pull tabs **the 1970s** are computer years for breweries, radical changes in the market lead to the first major brewery closures **1973** is the year of the first Beer Can Regatta in Darwin, Australia and **in 1978** the Can-Tiki (made of 15,000 cans) sails to Singapore **in 1975** cans get stay tabs – ring pulls riveted to the can **in 1986** the world's beer production rates reach the 1 billion hectoliter/gallon mark **in 1988** Czech Jaromir Vejvoda writes the Beer Barrel Polka (Roll out the barrel…) **in 1993** the largest bottle in the world (2.54 m, 625.5 l/8.3 feet, 165 gallons) is filled in Faversham, UK **in 1995** US breweries are allowed to include alcohol content on labels again after 60 years; UK brewers use genetically modified yeast **in 2000** the Boston Beer Company brews the strongest beer in the world, Samuel Adams Millennium, 20% alcohol by volume (abv).

Aroma...

1. AROMATIC, FRAGRANT, FRUITY, FLORAL
alcoholic:
spicy
vinous
solvent-like:
synthetic
lacquer-like
acetone
estery:
banana (ripe)
apple (ripe)
candy, glacial icy
fruity:
lemon
apple
banana
black currant
melon/green malt
pear
raspberry
strawberry
acetaldehyde:
green apple
green leaves
floral:
rose
geranium
carnation
perfumy
hoppy:
kettle hop
dry hop
hop flowers

2. RESINOUS TO GRASSY
resinous:
woody
nutty:
walnut-like
coconut-like
bean-like
almond-like
green like grass:
grassy
(freshly cut)
hay

3. GRAINY (RAW)
grainy:
straw, spelt
corn/semolina
(polenta)
malty:
malty
worty:
wort aroma

4. ROASTED
caramelized:
caramel
liquorice
burnt:
bread crust
roasted barley
smoked
phenolic:
tarry

5. CARBOLIC
carbolic:
tarry, carbolic

6. SOAPY, FATTY, OILY
fatty acid:
fatty, tallow
cheesy
sweaty
rancid butter
diacetyl:
buttery
caramel
rancid:
rancid oil
oily:
vegetable oil
mineral oil

7. SULFURY
sulphitic:
struck match
sulfury:
rotten egg
garlic
burnt rubber
prawn
cooked vegetables:
celeriac
fresh hay
charcoal
sweetcorn (cooked)
tomato (cooked)
onion
yeasty:
meaty

8. OXIDISED, STALE, MUSTY
overaged, catty:
sherry
madeira
catty
blackcurrant leaf
papery:
crispbread
papery
cardboardy
leathery:
leather-like
moldy:
earthy
musty

9. SOUR
sour, acidic:
sourness
vinegary
sour milk

10. SWEET
sweet:
honey
vanilla
jam
syrupy

11. SALTY
salty:
salty

Flavor

There are many different ways of describing the taste of beer:
balanced, broad, caramelly, clean, faded, finely bitter, full-bodied, hard, harmonious, heavy, light, malty flowered, malty perfumed, metallic, mild, non-cloying, oily finished, quickly fading, rich, rounded, satiating, smoky, smooth, soft, sticky, sweet, tangy, velvety, or yeasty…

Experts, beer tasters, and connoisseurs conduct sensory tests very systematically, in accordance with the European Brewery Convention (EBC) standard terminology, set out on the left-hand page. Similar to sensory testing of other products, the initial evaluation is done with the sensitive nose, before the tongue and gums actually taste the substance being analyzed. This is why very small samples are usually sufficient at beer tastings. If you swallow great gulps from huge glasses you will very quickly overtax and blunt your sense of taste.

almost pale

Pale, quick-dried malt makes very bright, pale beers, such as export or lager, which are known in Germany simply as "light beer", the rather less common ice beer is exceptionally pale in color

The visual side of beer is as important as flavor, for experience shows what the connoisseur knows, sees, and later tastes: soft, low-carbon **water** produces a paler beer; harder, carbon-rich water creates darker hues. However, the color of the beer in the

pale

Pale malts result in top-fermented, hoppy "kölsch" beers, as pale as "kristallweizen" (crystal wheat) or some pilsners

The color of

golden yellow

Beers that are brewed using pale pilsner malts turn out a deep gold in color, examples include some pilsners and pale ales and occasionally wheat beers

amber

This deep, warm color is characteristic of some "altbiers" and paler bocks, as well as festival beers produced for Oktoberfest, pale ale, and some wheat beers

glass is ultimately determined by the type and preparation of the malt, that is temperature and **kilning** time (drying process for the germinated barley). "Keep it cool and short for a paler sort, heat long and hot through for a darker hue". In fact, some

effects are only achieved by using a color malt. Experienced master brewers know all the tricks of the trade and are said to be able to go into a brewery **blindfold** and, based on the smell of the malt and liquid alone, say what color the resulting beer will be.

Typical of some ales, as well as "kölsch", pilsner, or what the Germans call a "cool blond" (freshly tapped beer)

Some wheat beers end up a deeper yellow, as do some "kölsch" beers or British pale ales on occasion

beer

black
Dark roasted and special

Infinite variety

The term beer is used for all drinks where the starch in a malty **base brew** is converted into sugar which yeast then turns into **alcohol**. However, ancient tricks of the brewing trade, as well as experience and **high-tech** equipment means that the world of beer teems with diversity.

Abbey and monastery beers

Regional beers which are produced in old monasteries and convents by nuns or monks or outside licensed breweries. The most famous are Belgium's Trappist beers.

Ale

Top-fermented beer originating in Britain, 3% to 11% abv, wide range of colors, and brewed according to old methods. Drunk at room temperature, low in carbon dioxide. Secondary fermented in the barrel or bottle it is a "real ale". Connoisseurs distinguish between brown ale, India pale ale (formerly drunk in the colonies, current boom in the US), mild ale (low alcohol), pale ale, English brown, old ale (very dark), bitter ale, cream ale (often blended with lager), and barley wine. Scottish ales are often darker, maltier and known as light, strong, export, or heavy (rather vinous). The best ales are regional specialties and are promoted by the Campaign for Real Ale.

Alt (old)

Traditional beer from the Lower Rhine area, approx. 4.8% abv, produced using an old (alt), top-fermentation method (no intensive cooling); overtones of hops and dark amber in color.

Barley wine

Special type of heavy, malty, top-fermented ale, over 6% abv, prized by connoisseurs as a "dessert beer".

Berliner Weiße

Top-fermented, slightly cloudy, sharp-tasting beer, 2.8% abv, brewed using barley and wheat malt. It is often drunk from goblet-shaped glasses, traditionally with a shot of woodruff or raspberry syrup and sipped through a straw.

Bitter (ale)

British standard beer, which at the time when hops were first used was considered a new type of "bitter". Low in carbonation and alcohol today, it tastes quite light and has become the most popular draught beer.

Bock

Bottom-fermented strong beer, originated in Einbeck in 1378 ("Ainpockisches Bier"), malty flavor and at least 7% abv. "May bock", "winter bock", and "festival bock" are brewed. Varieties with higher alcohol content are called "doppelbock" (double bock), the USA produces an even stronger "triple bock".

Dunkles (dark)

Bottom-fermented beer, 4.8% abv, a lager made darker by roasting the malt.

Export

Marketing name for pale (lager) beers from Germany, such as DAB and DUB, which have enjoyed success abroad.

Gueuze

Special type of Belgian lambic which uses wild yeasts and thereby produces a slightly vinous beer. Variations often include fruit in the fermentation process and extra carbon dioxide may be added.

Helles (light)

In German this usually means a lager, export, or pilsner with 4.6–5.6% abv, drunk as an alternative to "alt" or "schwarzbier".

Ice beer, Eisbier

Beer which is frozen using the ice rifing process and from which water is then removed, causing the aroma to become more concentrated, a stronger version is "ice bock".

Kölsch

Top-fermented beer, approx. 4.8% abv, only brewed in or around Cologne, served in pubs in tall slender 2cl/7 ounce glasses from huge round trays carried by waiters who are known as "Köbes".

Kriek

Fruity "gueuze" to which fermented cherries (kriek) are added, so more like a "kriek lambic".

Lager

Bottom-fermented (i.e. includes cooling) pale beer without the stronger pilsner hop content, often called "helles" (light). A more malty aromatic version is "dark lager". Keeps well, hence the name, "lager" = "store".

Lambic

Belgian beer which uses a proportion of raw wheat and is fermented with wild yeasts, named after the town of Lambeek. It matures in wooden barrels and gains a wine-like character and is often used to make the more sparkling "gueuze".

Märzen, Festbier, Wies'nbier

Bottom-fermented beer, 4–5% abv, formerly stored in icy cold caves, the special malt produces the mild, golden yellow or dark beer for the Oktoberfest.

Maize (corn) beer

Beer brewed using a malt with corn as a substitute for the barley or wheat.

Malzbier (malt beer)

Non-alcoholic, top-fermented beer (max. 0.5% abv), lightly hopped and sweet, its deep brown color comes from caramel.

Mild (ale)

Originating in Britain this is usually a dark ale. At 3–3.8% abv it is weaker and better value than dark ale or porter.

Millet beer

A beer from West Africa with a low alcohol content. The malt is made using millet as a substitute for wheat or barley.

Pilsner, pils

Most popular beer, the bottom-fermentation brewing technique was developed in the Czech town of Pilsen in 1842, it has now come to be brewed world-wide. Light, hoppy, tangy, finely foaming pale beer. Officially and in the USA it is a lager.

Porter

Bitter, hoppy beer with a strong roasted flavor, to which caramelized sugar is added. Very dark color and 6% abv. A lower alcohol content of 4.3% results in a lighter stout.

Rauchbier (smoked beer)

Beer made with malt which has been smoked over a wood fire and (like whisky) thereby acquires a smoky flavor.

Rice beer

A drink brewed using starch from rice as a malt substitute, it is also known as sake. Rice beer is 14–17% abv and is often mistakenly referred to as rice wine.

Roggenbier (rye beer)

Top-fermented beer which is brewed using rye malt instead of barley malt.

Root Beer

Very low-alcohol fermented drink made from herbs, spices, and sugar for the yeast, called "beer" for marketing reasons.

Schwarzbier (black beer)

Bottom-fermented beer, approx. 5% abv, brewed with very dark roasted malts.

Sorghum beer

Indo-African beer which is brewed from a malt that uses sorghum as a substitute for barley or wheat.

Stone beer

The product of very early brewing techniques, fire-heated stones were put into the mash, causing the malt to caramelize during secondary fermentation and giving a smoky flavor.

Stout

Slightly sweet beer with a strong (or stout) roasted flavor and dark brown color, 5–7.5 abv. Dry stout is less malty and is known all over the world as Guinness.

Trappist beers

Top-fermented strong beer from Belgium, it is now only brewed in six monasteries on an intentionally non-commercial basis.

Weizen, Weißbier (wheat beer)

Top-fermented, typically Bavarian beer, approx. 5.5% abv, with a fruity aroma. Made from equal quantities of wheat and barley malt, or sometimes just wheat malt. Secondary fermentation takes place in the bottle. Unfiltered it is "hefetrüb" (cloudy) or dark. When filtered it becomes kristall-weizen (crystal wheat).

Expectation

In many countries a firm head of foam at the top of the glass is traditionally expected. It is chiefly (but not solely) dependent on the protein content of the barley and the bitterness of the hops used

Disappointment

If the foam head disintegrates too quickly, there is something wrong with the beer underneath, causing an increase in the surface tension. This may be due to the water or an excessively high pH value of the mash or it could be the barley or the fault of the bitters

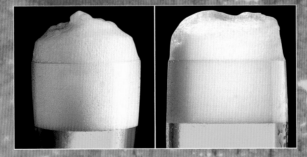

The crowning glory
Foam

If you order a swift ale in Britain, it will come quickly too – and with almost no head. The carbon dioxide produced in the ale barrel through secondary fermentation is enough to make the beer refreshing, but not to create a real head. In other countries, a towering **foamy head** is considered a challenge by brewmasters who know that protein, isohumulone, a higher alcohol content, and bitters are essential for the head, as they are **surface active.**

They form an elastic, cohesive film around each bubble of carbon dioxide, and polypeptide chains between the foam lamellas hold everything together. This tight-knit structure means a good head lasts a long time, prevents the carbon dioxide underneath from escaping, keeps the beer **fresh,** and also holds together as it gradually sinks sip by sip to the bottom of the glass. The **durability** of the froth shows the quality of the beer.

Crown caps

The densely pleated rim of this Korean cap ensures a firm, airtight fit round the neck of the bottle

If the cap fits...

It is carbon dioxide that makes beer such a sparkling, appetizing thirst quencher and beer drinking a **pleasure** right down to the last sweet sip. Once out of the cask, beer quickly goes flat; in bottles and cans it can last a long time. Some Trappist and specialty beers are **corked** and wired as decoratively as champagne bottles. With a swing-top bottle, the stopper is held in place with thick wire arms and when it is released it opens with a "pling" or a "plong" – **music** to the ears of nostalgic beer-lovers. When crown caps are removed there is a real hiss and they have a more socially acceptable, drink-from-the-glass **image**.

Bottle opener

The crown cap has inspired generations of inventors to make endless modifications and improvements to bottle openers. Some just want to devise the most ingenious way to remove the close-fitting cap

Essential companion

It's Murphy's Law that the bottle opener is never to hand when it's needed. The answer – a hole to tie a piece of string through

Appearance counts

A beer must be able to show off its color and head and the glass should entice the drinker to raise it to his or her mouth. Special glasses have been developed for every type of beer, but most important is always how the head is affected

Wheat beer glass

A glass with this waistline allows the bottle to be inserted upside down and removed slowly, thereby forming the foamy head. This trick of slowly pulling the bottle out has long been a ritual for wheat beer aficionados and still presents a frothy challenge to novices

Tankard

In this modern, very slender version of the classic beer tankard the beer on the table, with a foaming head the size of a handbreadth, is really eye-catching, and the head is easy to manage when filling the glass or holding it at an angle

Tulip glass

This exaggerated, ultra-slender shape is ideal for extra long drafts, because the foam sinks down towards the bottom right to the last mouthful

Beer tumbler

The universal beer glass made by Rastal. After the first few sips the rapidly sinking foam head is only slightly compressed and it is the ideal vessel for quick drinking

Beer goblet

A wide glass means the beer flows in generously as it is poured. The simple fullness of the glass and the color of its contents (light or dark) create a beautiful promise which should be fulfilled by the full-bodied flavor of the beer, right down to the bottom of such a goblet and the very last sip

Boot

In medieval times, mercenary soldier tradition required a man to be able to "take a boot", involving a nifty trick to avoid being drenched in beer

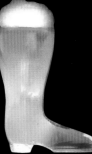

Form follows content

The glasses are as original as the beers. Faced with the breweries' vast range of exclusive glasses, collectors almost despair. Mindful of this and the different types of beer, **designers** create new custom goblets, unusual tulip glasses, special tumblers, and handy tankards. They consider the fact that glasses must be stable, **easily filled,** and should preserve the beer's crowning glory, the head. Good glasses don't widen towards the bottom, causing the foam to separate, instead the gradual narrowing of the glass means the **head** sinks elegantly to the bottom. Last but not least, the glass highlights the **color** of the beer, holding out the promise of cool refreshment.

Universal beer glass

Riedel Crystal of Kufstein is famous for mouth and machine-blown glasses for specific wines. For imparting full-bodied flavor, this shapely beer glass comes pretty close to the classic pilsner glass

With the advent of clear, bottom-fermented beer, it became the **custom** to drink from see-through glasses that are pleasing to the eye. Cloudy beers were better concealed in a non-transparent "stein". Even the big **tankards** that were traditionally brought to the table came to be made from glass. In the New World and Australia it is still usual to buy rounds in **pitchers** from which drinkers fill their own glasses.

Measures

Enjoy a jug

In America and increasingly elsewhere as well, the sociable thing to do is to buy a round of freshly-pulled beer in a jug so everyone can help themselves. It can be filled quickly, saves time at the bar and avoids complicated calculations with the bill

Brave a boot

Some people practice for the real boot tankard with a small boot-shaped glass, learning that the first air bubble that rushes into the upright toe area releases the remaining beer from a vacuum, causing it to slosh out over the drinker. Everyone takes a turn from the boot until some unlucky person who has not practiced is caught out. The trick is a sideways twist of the foot at the right moment

Pick a pitcher

In Australia downing cans of beer to beat the heat has almost become a ritual for the individual. However, a more sociable way to enjoy beer is from a pitcher like the one pictured here, because each person in the group takes it in turns to buy a round of 1.5 liters/3 pints of cool beer. Individual drinkers in civilized company prefer a stoneware jug or "stein". The 0.5 liters/1 pint of beer inside is protected by a lid with a decorative thumb rest

Grab a growler

During the last two centuries the sealable siphon (known as a growler) was the standard measure for fetching beer from the pub to drink at home. Recently brewpubs and microbreweries have resurrected this tradition and old collector's items have been updated to create handy siphons for transporting the popular take-away specialty beers

Too special to spill

Beer belongs in the glass but it doesn't always want to go in. The pressure in the cask or in old dispensing systems can mean lots of frustrating frothing, leading in some countries to the **cult of the foamy head** on top of an almost flat beer. Errors during bottling result in tiny bubbles which agitate the carbon dioxide when the can or bottle is opened, causing the beer to froth up and spill over. Heat and over-enthusiastic glass clinking also contributes. This as yet unresearched phenomenon is known as **gushing.**

Opened too quickly
When beer from bottles or cans spills over in an explosion of froth it is known as gushing. This is caused by tiny bubbles that mix with the carbon dioxide during bottling. These bubbles bring about the development of gas and when the pressure falls the entire content froths up

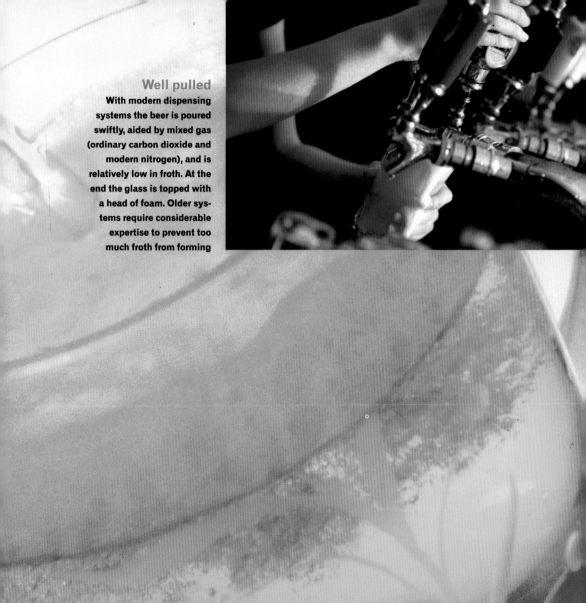

Well pulled

With modern dispensing systems the beer is poured swiftly, aided by mixed gas (ordinary carbon dioxide and modern nitrogen), and is relatively low in froth. At the end the glass is topped with a head of foam. Older systems require considerable expertise to prevent too much froth from forming

1.3 down in sec.

The world record for drinking a liter/quart of beer is held by Steven Petrosino from Carlisle, Pennsylvania, whose carefully trained gullet downed the beer in just 1.3 seconds in 1977. Apparently not a single drop was spilt. Since then, would be contenders for the record have had no luck, as the response of the "Guinness Book" of Records to any attempt is a definitive:

No!

Down in one

There is no magic in speed, neither is there any pleasure in downing beer, but men still like to do it for a bet. However, our mock-up photo must suffice here

WARNING!

Setting new beer drinking records or breaking old ones is no longer worth the effort. The "Guinness Book of Records" has stopped accepting applications or including entries for activities which could potentially endanger the drinker's health

The beer song

In 1935 two Berliners, Klaus Siegfried Richter (lyrics) and Wiga Gabriel, composed the famous drinking song. Few people know the verses but everyone joins in with the chorus and the punchline: "Oans, zwoa, gsuffa" (One, two, down the hatch!)

Gruß aus dem Kgl. Hofbräuhaus
MÜNCHEN

Refrain
F

One, two,

In Mün — chen steht ein Hof — bräu - haus,

f

For many people it is the best place in the world for beer. Over 400 years of tradition, a public house since 1828, bearer of the "HB" trademark since 1879, the Hofbräuhaus has seats for 2,800 and another 720 outside and in the beer garden. There are 5,000 regulars,

100 "Stammtische" (regulars' tables) and 425 guests of honor entitled to keep their personal tankards in the "tankard safe". Since 1935 the anthem of all beer-loving Bavarians has conjured up the inn's main purpose:

down the hatch!

"In Mun- / ich / is / the Hof- / bräu- / haus…"

1.
Down where the River Isar flows,
where "Grüß Gott"s are their hellos,
there's my darling Munich town,
nothing like it have I found.
Water is cheap and clean and good,
But it tends to thin the blood,
Better's a drop of golden wine,
But best of all and real fine:
  (Chorus)
  In Munich is the Hofbräuhaus:
  One, two, down the hatch…
  Barrel by barrel they drink it down:
  One, two, down the hatch…
  And now and then a worthy man:
  One, two, down the hatch…
  Showed just how much beer he could stand
  T'was early morning he began
  And late at night when he came out
  So great is the Hofbräuhaus.

2.
They don't drink beer there by the glass,
It's the realm of the tankard class!
And when the first tankard's downed,
Soon the next one comes around.
Back home the wife she gets a fright,
Where's her husband been all night?
But the good neighbors round about,
Know fine well and truth will out!
  (Chorus)

3.
Sure there are many other towns
Boasting lovely sights and sounds,
But one thing you'll find only here:
That is the fine Munich beer.
The singer of this little song
Has labored through the nights so long
Putting the beer here to the test
And Munich beer is the best.
  (Chorus)

Beer and lederhosen

It is a well-established cliché that lederhosen are to Bavaria what beer is to the tankard. In the film, "Bagdad Café", Brenda makes fun of this famous beer-drinking costume when she tries on a pair

The strong one

The one-syllable word "beer" has a one-syllable synonym – bock. This epitome of **strong beer** full of character has long since spread throughout the world and it is easy to forget that, like pilsner, the word was derived from a place name. In the Middle Ages large quantities of good beer were brewed in the half-timbered town of Einbeck, near Hanover, as it attracted large numbers of **pilgrims** who came to see the relic of the Savior's True Blood in the monastery chapel. The news of this special brew spread throughout Germany and the aristocracy became so fond of it that in 1615, quick to see a commercial opportunity, brewers in Munich began to produce it. It was then known as "einpöcksches" **strong beer** and later came to be called "bock". Traditionally it was 7% abv but master brewers began to produce ever stronger worts, in order to achieve a higher alcohol content. Logically, these

B**O**ck

strong beers were christened **"doppelbock".** In those days heavy beers could only be top-fermented, so they were brewed when it was cold and stored in icy caves. Consequently they were seasonal beers known as May bock, Christmas bock, or Lenten strong beers. Now any brewery can produce a bottom-fermented bock and so bocks can be golden, brown, or dark brown, with a high alcohol content and special flavors, depending on the malt and the brewer's preference. Bock beer ranges from malty sweet to very bitter, nowadays there are even bock and doppelbock wheat beers. Because Bavaria's doppelbocks are also good for Bavarian keg-openings and beer rituals during the **"strong beer season",** for centuries they have been given highly evocative names.

Many of them end in **-ator,** because the first bock was named by monks after the Savior ("Salvator"). Today the unmistakable strong beers produced by secular brewmasters bear names like "Kulminator", and the Aying Monastery is also known for its bock beers, including "Celebrator".

Packing a punch

A beer which has at least 7% alcohol with a 16% original wort can be called a "bock", named after Einbeck where it originated. The original bock, at 6.5% abv is by no means the strongest. In Germany the even stronger "doppelbocks" are often given expressive names ending in "-ator"

There is a great temptation for master brewers to try for an entry in the "Guinness Book of Records" with the "strongest beer in the world". Guinness's own Foreign Extra Stout is "only" 7.5% abv – not hard to beat in the intoxication stakes. Brewers and their yeasts coax the strength of the alcohol out of the wort. As a rule of thumb, dividing the original gravity of the wort by three gives an approximate idea of the eventual alcohol content. The Kulmbach EKU 28 turned its original gravity of 28 into 11% abv, the French Bière du Démon even

Power date Dec. 6th
The Schloss Eggenberg Brewery in Austria only brews its reddish brown 16% abv beer on the feast of St Nicholas (Samichlaus), it is then matured for ten months

managed 12% from 21.7. The stronger the wort the sweeter the end product. Austria's Samichlaus is a sweet Christmas beer which is 14% abv. A higher alcohol content than this requires lots of tricks to prevent the yeast from perishing in the high-alcohol brewing environment. Swabian brewmaster, Bernd Scheurle, of the Boston Beer Company, rose to the challenge. His highly sweetened wort contained maple syrup and had an original gravity of 37. The end result was the 17% abv. Samuel Adams Triple Bock. In 1999 he teased his yeast into producing a 20% beer, the as yet unbeaten Millennium ($200 "per bottle").

HERKULES·BIER
aus dem Hasenbräu-Augsburg

Power myth

Beer brewers have been competing for centuries to produce the "strongest" beer, for there is no better marketing slogan than being able to claim to be the Hercules of beers, a title currently held by the 20% abv Samuel Adams "Millennium"

% abv

The Belgian brew

Although small, Belgium is a beer paradise where hoppy monastery beers vie with imitators and original specialty beers. Strength is denoted by cap color and the vast range of different bottles delights collectors. Connoisseurs love the often devilishly strong beers of the pious Trappists

CHIMAY
PÈRES TRAPPISTES

PAR LES PÈRES TRA

Judas

BELGIAN GOLDEN ALE

ks kruiken

PRODUCT OF BEL

Alc. 8%vol.
e 33 cl

Collines
zelloise

Cerveza Extra

LLES - (068) 54 31 6

Bière
Belge

BRUN

"Refreshes the parts other drinks can't reach", to paraphrase an old advertising slogan. Thirst is actually a physical signal to be taken seriously. The fact that the body needs **2.7 liters/2.8 quarts** of water every day is used by some to justify consuming this volume in beer. However, doctors see our passion for alcohol as a **"luxury thirst"** because just one liter of beer of average alcohol content means hours of hard work for many different organs. Each liter is systematically processed, digested, filtered, and its constituent parts and calories used, but more alcohol always

Cause and effect

gets into the **bloodstream.** In moderation alcohol only slows down the central **nervous system,** making the drinker more cheerful or even unhappy. In large amounts alcohol increasingly impedes our control mechanisms. Drinking spirits with beer or having beer cocktails amplifies all these effects. The diligent but slow liver then has a hard job **sobering up.**

getting high
Alcohol molecules are fat and water soluble and penetrate all areas of the body, quickly reaching the brain, inhibiting active neurons, and dulling the central nervous system within 10 to 20 minutes

reaction
The first alcohol effects come after 20 minutes, with the maximum effect after another 20. This lasts for about two hours, noticeably altering reactions, even to the extent of loss of motor control

absorption
The stomach lining soaks up 20% of the alcohol, the small intestine absorbs the rest into the blood

amplified
Drinking a schnapps takes otherwise harmless beers to the alcohol borderline, like this dexterous "double decker", for example

drinking
Thirst is natural; an urge for alcohol is a "luxury thirst" and even the very first sips dull the tastebuds

swallowing
A trained larynx willingly opens the entrance to the 25-cm/10 inch-long gullet to swill down the contents of the drinker's glass

filling up
The upper half of the stomach fulfils a depot function, holding 1.5 to 2 liters/3 to 4 pints of beer, and can expand further with no tangible strain

processing
About 95% of the alcohol is broken down by the hard-working liver at 10 to 20 milliliters/0.3 to 0.6 ounces per hour, just 2% is processed by the kidneys, the rest is exhaled or perspired

disposal
Of the 180 liters/47.5 gallons filtered every day, the kidneys have to expel 1.5 liters/3 pints; with just 200ml/7 ounces, the urge to urinate comes from the bladder

Beer belly: full of beer

Since the paunch trend was superseded by the desire for a honed **washboard stomach,** many people have argued and held forth against the beer belly. Brewers and their most enthusiastic customers merely see that a large proportion of the alcohol calories are canceled out as the liquid carbohydrates are broken down. Dieticians reliably claim that a pure **diet of beer** with no additional solid food would actually make us slim. Doctors are searching for an **AC enzyme** which may pre-program some men for belly fat. Therefore gene type would partly determine whether a beer lover could proudly wear the **"Beer formed my lovely body"** T-shirt across his paunch. The 400–500 calories in each liter of beer drunk might not be enough to make you fat – but they could start to get you addicted...

Unresolved dispute

There is still no definitive answer as to what makes you fatter – tankard or plate. However, beer does make you hungry and both together certainly develops a belly

and full of pride

Manly pride: The symbol of prosperity that is the beer belly, formed through regular beer drinking and overeating, may in fact be due to a genetically weak enzyme in fat cell growth

Beer pilgrims

Since the Church long ago conceded that beer did not break the fast, **monastery breweries** prospered. Some still produce beer today – Belgium's Trappists enjoy international success and Germany's Andechs Monastery has run popular pubs since 1455. Then there are smaller monasteries like Mallersdorf where brewmistress, **Sister Doris,** produces just 3,000 hecto-liters/approx. 800,000 gallons, a fifth of which is consumed by the nuns and staff. Monastery beers are popular with travelers, but the real places of pilgrimage are Munich's Hofbräuhaus and the old brew cellar beer halls at the birthplace of pilsner – **Plzen (Pilsen)** in the Czech Republic. On October 5th the brewery here hosts a festival to celebrate the famous beer. Beer fans flock to **Budejovice** in Eastern Bohemia for the original European "Budweiser Budvar". A dispute with US rival Anheuser Busch over the "Bud" name has raged since 1875.

Volkstracht aus der Umgebung.

TOTALANSICHT

GRUSS aus PILSEN

aus 16. Nov. 1900

Verlag von Jos. Milt in Pilsen.

Prosit Gurgel —
Jetzt kommt ein Wolkenbruch.

BUDWEIS. — Totalansicht.

Touching scenes

Andechs Monastery on the "Holy Mountain" near Munich looks almost as idyllic today as the panorama over the Czech town of Plzeň in 1900 or the view of the Black Tower in the royal town of Budejovice – but the excesses of earlier beer pilgrims are a thing of the past

Swigging scenes

Drowning their sorrows

Beer helps revive flagging spirits at the end of the football day in "When Saturday comes" (1996) and provides consolation to abandoned father, Daniel Hillard (Robin Williams), who gets himself hired by his ex-wife as nanny "Mrs Doubtfire"

Beer is as ubiquitous on film as it is in everyday life. It comes over well in color films and finds a place in all manner of **scenes,** from people talking over a glass or two to the image of the lone drinker drowning their sorrows. In films we see how beer drinking is inextricably linked with **body language.** How someone reaches for the bottle or holds a glass **speaks volumes** about their state of mind. Only smoking, another activity that is focused around the head, gives as much away.

beer on film

Deutsch courage

Full of self-irony, actor Gerhard Polt clings to his beer to boost his German confidence as Erwin Löffler in the film, "Man spricht deutsh" (1986), where he abandons himself to dreaming of an affair with an Italian woman on the beach at Terracina

Beer chancer

Meat Loaf is beer truck driver, Travis W. Redfish, who in the 1979 film "Roadie" becomes a roadie for groupie Lola and encounters Blondie over a beer

"If it's beer garden weather at ten o'clock…"
Southern Germans define beer garden weather as being if it is still 22 °C/71 °F at ten p.m. Then the debate about closing time really hots up.

"Beer paper is no urban myth"
Hand-made paper factory, Gmund, uses recycled bottle labels and the spent hops left over from beer production to make "beer paper". It comes in five classic shades: "wheat", "lager", "pils", "ale", and the dark "bock" – so all those who are truly dedicated to beer can express their thoughts on beer paper.

"Someone should set up a beer party…"
In 1991 a Beer Fans Party was founded in Poland. It was represented in the Sejm by 16 members of parliament and was committed to "economic progress". In Australia the Lower Excise Fuel and Beer Party called for numerous tax cuts, including on beer, while the aim of the Original Senkrechte Bierpartei in Graz, Austria, was to galvanize boozing buddies into action.

"Yuck supplement for a Dirty Scoundrel…"
In the area around Cologne Cathedral, a kölsch with cola, known elsewhere in the Rhine region as a Krefelder, is derogatorily called a Dirty Scoundrel. In some pubs drinkers must pay a 5-cent "yuck supplement" for this adulteration of the local beer.

"Bottleology is one word for it…"
Anyone who collects bottles of beer and never drinks them must be teetotal, strong-willed, or out to break a record like Peter Broeker of Geesthacht near Hamburg. His 12,548 bottles from 2,440 breweries, 40% of them from abroad, would stretch 3 km/1.9 miles laid end to end. There should be a better word than bottle collector for someone that dedicated – perhaps "bottleologist" or even "lagenologist".

"Harry Porter is Scandinavian…"
At Norway's annual champion homebrewer competition (Årets hjemmebrygg) in Oslo, Henrik Svalheim won first prize with a magnificent beer. However, he refused to reveal the secret of the magical wizard's brew he called "Harry Porter".

"Kobe cattle are beer guzzlers…"
The most expensive beer bellies in the world belong to Japanese Kobe cattle which, from the age of 20 months, are fed beer every day and massaged with sake, to increase fat content and create perfectly marbled meat. Ten months later they are the world's most expensive steaks. Now Kobe cattle are guzzling beer to create the luxury meat in France and the USA too.

"There are luxury beers…"
Fine, clear crystal wheat beer can no longer be called champagne wheat beer. French jealousy saw to that. But the problem has been remedied by a Swiss brewer who produces a beer "like wine" as was once

Bee

small

talk

made for the czar's court. The resulting dark, malty, porter-like Balik beer is matured in oak for two years and is recommended as an accompaniment to the Balik salmon already on the Swiss innovator's menu.

"Ölsund is a tax frontier…"

Because Swedes like to sail across the Öresund to Denmark, where they can buy lots of "øl" (beer) cheaper than at home, the sea between the two countries is now referred to as Ölsund rather than Öresund.

"Joe Bloggs or Sally Six-pack…"

Since the six-pack became such a successful product, its main consumers in the USA have come to be symbolized by it. The German equivalent of Joe Bloggs is Otto Normal Consumer or Erich or Erika Commonman – in the USA they have Joe Bloggs and Sally Six-pack.

"Monitor the drinking temperature of your beer…"

If beer is too cold it does not froth or taste right. In Germany the correct temperature is 4–9 °C/39–48 °F. The Cologne beer, "1396" (the year in which the people of Cologne freed themselves from patrician rule), has a "thermolabel" – if the beer is cooled to the right temperature a second "1396" appears on the label.

"Get your priorities right…"

The Finnish saga, Kalewala, has 200 verses devoted to the creation of the world and 400 verses about beer.

"Full Moon beer is illuminating…"

Gaps in the market must be filled – even for sleepwalkers. Full Moon beer is brewed just once a month by organic brewers near Lake Constance and in the Appenzell area of Switzerland. On moonlit nights sleepwalkers are meant to be mysteriously drawn to their fridges where they will find this beer.

No country in the beer-drinking world has such a well-preserved pub tradition as Britain. The British have been brewing their dark **bitter** since 1002. The oldest surviving inn is The Fighting Cocks in St Albans near London, which actually predates brewing in Britain. The Olde Trip to Jerusalem in Nottingham, conveniently situated on a pilgrimage route,

Endless variety:

The range of beer in free houses was never restricted and the law has now changed for pubs owned by breweries. Almost all pubs are proud of the traditional ales and maintain a wide selection

Make it a pint:

Beer always comes in pints or half pints, bought by the round in the pub. The beer is on draught, that is, lever pumps fill the glasses to the brim with only a small head, and you always pay straight away

the PU

tapped its first barrel in 1189. Because brewers in those days were monks, many pubs have rather pious names. The more comical names came later, as did the division of the pub into the proletarian **public house** (hence pub) and the somewhat more refined saloon, befitting the still flourishing class society. Late opening, closing in the middle of the day, and the far too early **closing time** were intended to have an edifying effect and the system was only liberalized at the end of the 20th century. British society developed its own pub rituals: whatever you order you pay for straight away;there are no moody bar staff; it is an unwritten rule that religion and politics are never discussed in pubs – the ever-important

J B

weather has to do instead. Finally, it is a matter of honor that each person in a group takes it in turns to buy **a round** – especially since each pub carries an original range of beers and offers a changing selection of special (often local) ales. This newly rediscovered love for ale is represented by the nationwide Campaign for Real Ale (CAMRA).

Atmosphere:
Historic and themed pubs are very popular. In London's Dirty Dick's an 18th-century legend has been resurrected which claims that the pub became so charmingly dilapidated after the death of the landlord's fiancée

Last orders:
Britain's pub laws are strict, but before closing time, proclaimed at the top of the landlord's voice, you can finish your "last orders" beer and your game of darts. The laws are different in Scotland

Three Guinness,

The most famous stout in the world comes from Ireland and its complexion, full-bodied flavor, and coffee notes betray the fact that Arthur Guinness started off in 1759 as a brewer of porter, from which he developed the classic **dry stout.** Guinness is famous for the fine foaming head on top of the lightly cooled beer. Guinness was a pioneer in the introduction of "mixed gas", where rapidly evaporated nitrogen briefly swirls up the carbon dioxide. This effect is produced in bottles and cans by a **widget** – on opening the fall in pressure activates a ball containing the gas.

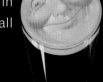

please!

ZOOZIE'Z
VIKING-PILS

Acceptance

Drinking under the summer sun until there is no more space on the table for the glasses. Male drinking rituals come with the excuse that everyone must have some fun – and for lots of fun you need lots of beer

Tolerance

A man does not allow himself to be interrupted with his beer. Once he has decided to open a barrel, he is as faithful to it as to his own wife – and that has been true since Hagar's Viking times

Boys and

Beer means hours of relaxed chatting over moderate amounts of alcohol. In more authoritarian times men saw their beer sessions as a **privilege,** maintained through avidly practiced, enthusiastically handed-down rituals. Groups of students, single men, and young people still preserve the art of "drinking contests" with almost archaic passion. The male "us feeling" of **group beer-drinking** ensures acceptance within the group and outside it. Thus, there are established routines governing round-buying and glass-clinking etiquette, tests of courage and drinking stamina, and **bonding** over a beer.

their beer

Temptress

In the early days of advertising women and beer went well together – so long as the cool blonde beer was in the foreground with the sporty blonde behind promising good cheer

A beer for

Once upon a time beer meant flirting – with the landlady or a busty barmaid dressed in a low-cut blouse. But this traditionally boozy, male-dominated realm is gradually losing its former **image.** Increasingly, women enjoy sitting and having a beer together and so old habits and attitudes to the **"wench"** have had to change. In Germany alone, one in three glasses of beer is drunk by a woman and these new beer drinkers tend to know what they do and don't like, leading

the ladies...

Flirtiness

Since in Germany, nation of beer-lovers, every third beer drinker is female, more and more women can be seen flirting with this new image in adverts and doing it for real at the bar

to a growth in the market for specialty beers. They appreciate **beer aesthetics,** love unusually shaped glasses, and want something more than the standard beer. This trend has made beer less masculine and introduced more equality to the flirting at the bar. After all, don't forget that in France and Italy the words "bière" and "birra" are **feminine** nouns…

Waitress

Generations of men who grew up with the image of the flirty barmaid who ably demonstrates her beer-handling skills as she cheerfully brings over the refills

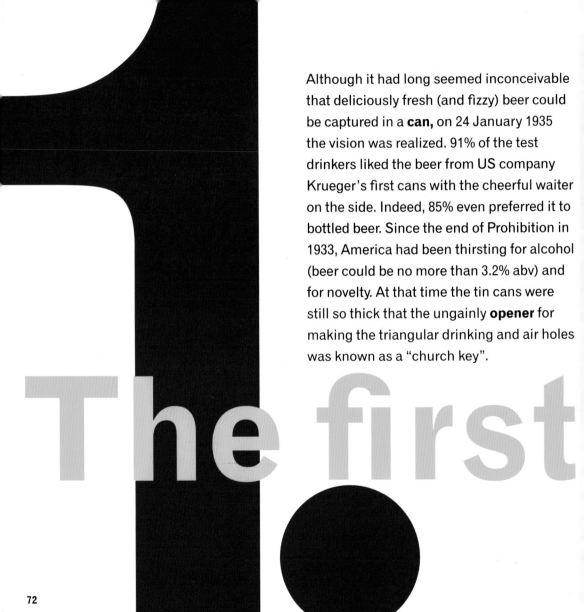

Although it had long seemed inconceivable that deliciously fresh (and fizzy) beer could be captured in a **can,** on 24 January 1935 the vision was realized. 91% of the test drinkers liked the beer from US company Krueger's first cans with the cheerful waiter on the side. Indeed, 85% even preferred it to bottled beer. Since the end of Prohibition in 1933, America had been thirsting for alcohol (beer could be no more than 3.2% abv) and for novelty. At that time the tin cans were still so thick that the ungainly **opener** for making the triangular drinking and air holes was known as a "church key".

1

The first

12 FL. OZ. SAME AS BOTTLE

KRUEGER'S
Finest
BEER

COOL BEFORE SERVING
INTERNAL REVENUE TAX PAID

1935

Beer drinkers in Richmond, Virginia, were test drinkers for the first beer in a can made by the Krueger Brewing Company of Newark, NJ, but back then the canned cream ale still required a tin opener

Soon there were cans with bottleneck-style tops and screw caps. Eventually, the removable **pull tab** was introduced in 1963, followed by the more environmentally friendly stay tab. US soldiers brought the innovative cans to Europe and from the 1950s the public quickly became accustomed to the handy drink-and-throw-away **beer can.** The opening hiss of the can soon became a popular sound.

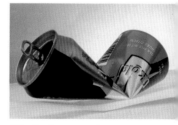

Drink and throw away

If it was not for empty beer cans many boys would never have started playing football. But in 2003 Germany introduced a deposit on cans

2.173

1,350 m.p.h.

BRITISH AIRWAYS

A beer, please
Fuller's multiple prize-winning, well-balanced bitter is considered to be so delicately hoppy and mildly malty that drinking it is like "angels dancing on your tongue". The London brewery was proud to quench the thirst of British Airways Concorde passengers at supersonic speeds

FULLERS
LONDON
PRIDE
Outstanding

STELLA
ARTOIS

Une bière, s.v.p.
The Belgian pilsner has been a mildly bitter star since 1926 and is famous far beyond the boundaries of the country where it is brewed. It took off with Air France's Concorde and was served to passengers 18 km/11 miles up in the stratosphere

km/h

The fastest beers

From 1973 the fastest way to cross the Atlantic was by Concorde. Flying at more than twice the speed of sound, the 62-metre/68 yards-long plane got so hot that it became 15 to 20 centimeters/6 to 8 inches longer. A good cooling system inside the plane was therefore essential – for the passengers, the obligatory champagne, and also for the ice-cold beer.

G-BOAC

Old Europe taught the art of brewing to the New World, which reciprocated with better marketing and **packaging ideas.** Back in the 1930s beer cans were already common in the USA – "doubles", "fours", and sixer "hom-paks". GIs yearned for them in Europe and provoked a boom in the handy packaging. **Progress** also meant the end of wooden barrels, when the more stable and hygienic aluminum kegs robbed beer cellars of their romanticism and the descendent of the gallon jug became known as the six-pack.

From barrel to six-pack

Stack 'em up

In the old wooden crates the weight of the stack was borne by the bottlenecks. Only since the 1980s have bottles, standardized right down to their crown caps, been stored in stackable crates. Initially they were all the same but breweries now have their own, usually brightly colored, designs

Take-away

Since around 1970, the popularity of the six-pack has grown in Europe – the handy half dozen can be picked up on a quick shopping trip and is an essential element for spontaneous parties

It does not take long to drink a beer but the thirst for brands is insatiable. Names and logos adorn **cult objects** in seemingly endless quirky variety. Throughout the world, the most popular beer novelties are toys. Children in the developing world make highly original, incredibly detailed cars from beer cans, children in the so-called First World have perfect mini-trucks or freight cars for their model railways, usually chosen by their brand-loyal fathers. **Recycling** has led to the creation of more "feminine" objects, such as decorative crown cap handbags.

Toying with cr

Beer Beetle

Imaginative Africans use metal shears and pliers to fashion whole fleets of vehicles from the most decorative beer cans. This Beetle would cost a collector a couple of dollars and feed its creator for several days

Can truck

There are plenty of life-size versions of this miniature beer truck in Africa, for the major brands have long been quenching thirst world-wide. The cans are reincarnated as items for collectors and "beerologists"

eativity

Beer freight car

Grown-up children still like playing with trains and all the model railway firms and many breweries produce beautifully decorated beer freight cars aimed at this target group. These additions to the rolling stock make popular gifts and are fanatically collected

Bottletop bag

These bags, which are decorated with used crown caps, are made in Kenya and then lined with fine leather in Europe by Mulberry. Inspired by the son of the company's president, all profits go to fund **AIDS** education initiatives in **Africa**

drink, swallow

booze · brourg · gl · glog · glop · glork

glou · gloub · gloup · glp · gluck · glunk

glut · gulb · gulp · slurp · unk · quaff · slobber

burp

beurp · blurp · burp · hops

belch · üülps · urp · grunt

hiccup

hic · hick · hicks · hip · hips

slurp, lick

glork · gluck · glurg · lick · slurk · smurp

spit, spew, vomit, throw up

barf · beuark · retch sputter · beurkgll-glleurkgl · brr · brrrfffj · brrrfjzzzz

Speech bubble beer

FUMP

Almost every aspect of beer has been researched, even the world of **comic strip** drinkers. Sociologists and linguists exploring this highly specialized field are fascinated by the way speech bubbles and expressive words are used to bring the silent cartoon world to tumultuous life. These onomatopoeic words are invented and embellished by cartoonists and translators. Many have become internationally established as the sounds for bottle-opening, glass-clinking, or burping, thereby facilitating international sales. German cartoonist, Brösel, invented an extra special **brew** for his beer-loving comic hero, Werner, and for the all-important starting signal he came up with the word **FUMP.**

Tops away!
For German comic hero, Werner, the sound of the flip-top bottle opening is the most beautiful in the world . It has since become a marketing gag of the Flensburg Brewery

On the mat

Beer mats were first used on top of glasses but from 1892 they were put beneath overflowing glasses. Since then they have been used for writing notes, exciting **collectors,** tallying beers consumed, or even as puzzles for lonely beer drinkers like Yvan Attal in "My wife is an actress". Tormented by jealousy, he builds a fragile house of illusions.

Beer makes you hungry and is a great accompaniment to food. Not just Bavarian-style with **haxn** or **hendl,** for many restaurants and chefs have their favorite "cooking beer". Dark beer is perfect for pepping up marinated beef, wheat beer sauce wafts aromatically around tender lamb beneath a herb crust, and a **pilsner sauce** truly ennobles roast breast of guinea fowl with spinach. Nutritious beers make an excellent marinade for oxtail, knuckle of veal can be marinated in **beer wort,** and bread dough made from spent hops seals the juices into baked ham. In Bavaria beer is even used in desserts: for frozen raspberry charlotte with frothy beer liqueur sauce or frozen "bock beer zabaglione". The Aying brewery restaurant even serves **"Beeramisu".**

Beer accompaniment

Fishy

Beer makes you hungry and its full-bodied flavor is a match for the heartiest fare. The best accompaniment to beer is "matjes" (young herring). Like beer, they contain so many elements that are good for the liver after a boozy night that both together form the perfect hangover breakfast

Snacks

Well-salted slices of radish or crunchy whole radishes may not fill you up but they do make you thirsty. No wonder they are sold in some beer gardens for next to nothing

Saucy

Every beer has its own character and chefs who recognize this know how to bring it out in their cooking. Reduction intensifies the individual aromas which imbue sauces with interesting hoppy flavors or, cooked on a higher heat, produce a tasty maltiness

Just a dash

A dash of beer added to a rich joint of pork with sauté potatoes enhances the flavor because, depending on temperature and length of cooking, the malt in the liquid or on the crackling caramelizes into a piquant sweetness. The type of beer used is important – as is the beer chosen to accompany the meal

Specialty

Hops and malt are not the only things that can make **water** taste good. Before the effects of yeast were properly understood, beer was flavored with oak bark, gale, or sloes. As beers became purer and clearer, so the appeal grew of enhancing the hint of **sweet-**

Going to the dogs

Fruit-flavored beers are brewed like beer, but with lemon they taste like lemonade and Kriek is like cherry juice. CB has a hint of euphoria and Halloween has pumpkin soup notes

ness with a little **"shot"** of something to produce a definite flavor. Most **fruit** work well and even coffee and cocoa are sometimes used to round off the brew, or tangy lemon is added for a "Mexican" flair. Brewers and enthusiasts have never stopped experimenting to find the ultimate **kick.** The healthy hemp beer only contains the legal, industrially cultivated plant.

beers

Garnished with banana

You get apple, pear, mango, chestnut, and even oyster, coffee, or chocolate beers, so why not add banana (after all it tastes good) in the same way as aniseed, juniper, caraway, or bayleaves were once used?

Turned on its head

Peat-smoked barley flavors this **Scottish** whisky beer while the **Baltic** brew is sweetened with honey

ADELSCOTT

The Di...

ADELSCOTT
Beer with
Whisky Malt

LITHUANIAN
AVILYS
HONEY
BEER

CHAPEAU
banana
LAMBIC

Beer cocktails, devised and served by imaginative bar staff with a flair for the unusual, are becoming ever more popular. In most cases the taste of the beer is changed and enhanced, while others simply amplify the alcoholic effect. The **amusing names** for these "altered" beers are often traditional or regionally connected but rarely deadly serious.

Lemon Shandy

Radler

Beer

Altbier Punch
Altbier + cola + grenadine + tinned fruit

Amer Bière
4:1 Amer Picon + lime juice + cold lager

Bavaria
Lager + peppermint syrup + lime juice

Beer Breezer
Lager + vodka + Tabasco + celery salt

Beer Buster
Lager + vodka + Tabasco

Beer Floatie
Lager + ice cream + rootbeer + schnapps

Beer, mexican style
Lager + salt + lemon

Beer-A-Lade
Lager + Gatorade + maple syrup + Tabasco

Beeraquirilla
Lager + tequila + rum + Daiquiri- + Margarita mix + ice

Beerdriver
Lager + vodka taste + orange juice

Benzin, Beer Buster
Lager + vodka

Berliner Weisse with a shot
Berliner Weisse + fruit syrup

Berliner Weisse extra
Fruit syrup + corn schnapps

Bismarck
Dark beer + very dry sparkling wine

Black & Tan
Guinness + pale ale or lager

Black & Red, Black & Sweet, Black Cherry
Guinness + Kriek

Black Brother/ Death/ Monk
Guinness + Trappist beer

Black Fog
Stout + raspberry liqueur

88

Black Russian
Guinness + vodka

Black Silky Knickers
Guinness + whiskey + Dry Blackthorn

Black Velvet
Guinness + champagne

Black Velvet 2
Lager + Rum

Black Velveteen
Lager + Cider

Boiler Maker
Lager + whisky

Brown Betty
Ale + brandy, hot

Cheap Jakob
Lager + sparkling wine

Chti'cass
Lager + Cassis

Churchill
Lager + Campari

Coachman's tipple
1:2 red vermouth + Campari + Angostura, top up with export

Cythum
Lager + Houlle genever gin

Diesel
Lager + cola

Diplomat
Dark beer + champagne or sparkling wine

Dog's Nose
Bitter ale + gin

Golden Cream
Guinness + vanilla ice cream (Guinness in first!)

Green Wave
Vodka spritzer + 2 cl/7 ounces Blue Curaçao, stir, top up with lager

Guinness Cooler
Dubonnet + Kahlua + Cointreau, top up with Guinness, stir until frothy

Isar Water, Isarmass
Wheat beer + Blue Curaçao + apple or orange juice

Jean Bière
at least 1cl/3.5 ounces cognac + lager

Krefelder
Alt or lager + cola

Lady's Beer
1cl/3.5 ounces rum + cherry juice + 6cl/21 ounces cream + bock beer

Lager-Lime
Lager + lime juice

Lemon Shandy, Radler
Lager + lemonade

Loyal Man
Lager + cola

Midnight, Velvet Pussy
Guinness + port

Nord Express
Lager + Cassis + lime juice

Poor-man's Black Velvet
Guinness + cider, sometimes with Cassis

Purple Meany
1:1 Guinness + bitter + cassis

Rafraichissement
5:2 wheat beer + sparkling wine

Russ
Wheat beer + lemon-ade

Shandy Gaff
Lager + ginger ale

Snake Bite
Lager + cider

Tango Panaché
Lager + lemonade + grenadine

Tovarish
Juice of 1/2 lemon + 4cl/14 ounces vodka + 0.3l/10 ounces strong beer

Tulip
Lager + genever gin

Black & Tan

Black Velvet

Berliner Weisse

In high spirits

When a soccer player like **FC Bayern Munich's Giovane Elber** spontaneously douses a victor like coach Ottmar Hitzfeld, in a burst of high spirits, it does not have to be with champagne. If there are no magnums around, a goblet or giant glass of beer will do. In any case, beer is good for the hair and, used externally, it can have excellent cosmetic effects

Foaming: a drop of hea

Plenty is already known about the internal "application" of beer but its **external** use is often neglected. Aficionados recommend using beer as a shampoo to regenerate and fortify the hair and give it body and shine. **Natural beauticians** even advocate a recipe involving an egg yolk stirred into 50ml/ 1.6 ounces of beer, with a tablespoon of rum to improve circulation and three drops of chamomile oil to round off the concoction. Beer contains so much **vitamin B** and, as well as minerals, so many proteins, that its thick foam can even be used to make an excellent face mask. In addition to the usual method of imbibing beer, some people prefer to adopt a more concentrated approach to its **internal** use. They take brewer's yeast in **tablet form,** complementing their vitamin intake at the same time as providing nourishment for the liver, soothing their skin, invigorating their metabolism and, as luck would have it, helping to repel **midges.**

In yeast form

Brewer's yeast tablets work wonders – good for the skin and bowels and are as a vitamin-rich nutritional supplement

Capillary treatment

Beer shampoo provides beer proteins and vitamin B for fine, soft hair, has an astringent effect on the cell membranes of a scalp damaged by dandruff, and gives hair body and shine

lthy beer for the head

Festivals

All year round and all around the world beer fans gather in tents or vast decorated halls for beer tasting events or, more popularly, to down it by the **jug.** Throughout the world, countless "Oktoberfests" are organized locally, with Bavarian specialties and following Munich traditions. But the Munich Oktoberfest still rivals them all.

here:

low-alcohol beer is less than 1.5% abv, no beer is completely alcohol-free ("non-alcoholic" beer is still 0.5% abv and in France it is as much as 1% abv)

tapping the barrel is when the barrel is opened or "tapped", when the beer and carbon dioxide lines are brought together and the beer starts to flow

beer defects result from beer being infected with harmful germs, including acetobacteria or lactobacilli which lead to flavor defects

beer additives, such as rice, corn, and sugar, are permitted in the EU and world-wide, but Germany still has the Purity Law, albeit now optional

bitter is the characteristic beer flavor, it should be imparted by the hops alone but is sometimes a beer defect due to protein or yeast bitterness

Thirst for knowledge

Landlords have some knowledge, the label on the bottle does not tell you everything, but you can learn something new with every beer. Those things you do know you will be able detect in your beer – be it fact or interpretation.

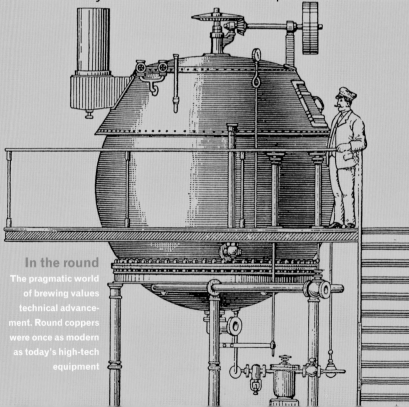

In the round
The pragmatic world of brewing values technical advancement. Round coppers were once as modern as today's high-tech equipment

head the foam on top of a freshly poured beer

organic beer is brewed from non-chemical and non-GM ingredients often sourced locally

diet beer is bottom-fermented beer, 4–5% abv, where carbo-hydrates have been fermented out, dry and very hoppy

line measure is the line on the glass denoting the standard measure

Festbier (festival beer) is a light, sweet, full-bodied beer brewed for special events, e.g. Munich Oktoberfest

GM beer may ultimately be unavoidable as there are already experiments world-wide with GM yeast and corn varieties

tannic acid, like the bitterness and hop oil, comes from the lupulin granules in female hop flowers

gushing occurs when tiny bubbles (due to

a fault in the bottling process) cause all the carbon dioxide to be released at once and the beer to overflow when the bottle or can is opened

carbon dioxide is the refreshing part of the beer, formed with the alcohol during fermen-tation and often used as the pressurizing gas in the dispensing system

longnecks have been popular since it became trendy in the 1980s to drink some beer from the bottle

Malzbier is malt beer, a sugary, top-fermented beer which is unfer-mented (less than 0.5% abv) and is dark-colored due to the caramel content

Märzen is a traditional, strong beer, brewed light and sweet for the summer, now usually as Oktoberfest beer

Mass is the old Bavarian beer measure, origi-nally 0.72l/1.2 pints

plus lots of foam, now legally defined as 1l/2 pints with the foam

top-fermenting is the old art of brewing at 15–20°C/59–68°F with yeasts (sacchromyces cerevisiae) rising to the surface at the end of fermentation (kölsch, alt, Berliner weisse, wheat beer)

Reinheitsgebot is the Purity Law (beer may contain only hops, barley, and water) in-troduced in Bavaria by Duke Wilhelm IV in 1516, to the whole of Germany in 1906 and abolished by the EU in 1987, since then optional

nitrogen is used in beer transportation, dispensing systems, cans, and bottles to maintain pressure, disperses quickly and swirls the carbon dioxide attractively

original wort is the malt content in unferment-ed beer, or wort, which varies between 6% and 25%; during fermenta-

tion the yeast turns it into 1/3 alcohol and 1/3 carbon dioxide, the rest remains unfer-mented. The higher the original wort, the stronger the beer (rule of thumb: original wort divided by 3 = abv)

stein is the traditional tankard, historically made of stoneware, now glass, often a highly decorative collector's item

siphon is a jug with a swing stopper used to transport beer

bottom-fermenting is brewing at 4–9°C/39–48°F, the yeast (saccharomyces carls-bergensis) sinks to the bottom after fermen-tation; widespread since the late 19th century with industrial cooling processes for longer-lasting lagers, pilsners, exports, and bocks

alcohol by volume, abv, is the percentage of pure alcohol in a liter of beer

Final word

"The mouth of a perfectly happy man is filled with beer", the Ancient Egyptians enthused. In the Christian West some saw beer as a sign that God loved his people and wanted to see them happy. Germans like to quote an aphorism which has it that a beer which is not drunk has failed in its purpose. An American actor actually once confessed that, upon reading about the evils of drinking, he immediately gave up reading

Web of knowledge

www.allaboutbeer.com

www.beerhunter.com

www.beerme.com

www.beertown.org

www.bierboerse.com

www.biersuche.com

www.brauer-bund.de

www.camra.org.uk

www.deutschlands-brauereien.de

www.ibv1958.de

Picture credits

The editor and publishers would like to thank the archives, companies, and photographers for authorizing picture reproduction and for their kind support:

AKG 8 (top l.), 9 (bottom l.), 18 l., 51; action press 8 (bottom r.); Prof. Werner Back 13; Günter Beer 54; Britain on View/ BTA 18 center, 64 (3), 65 (2); Budweiser Budvar 8 (top center); Bulls Press 68 bottom, 69 bottom; Gesellschaft für Öffentlichkeitsarbeit der Deutschen Brauwirtschaft e.V. 12 (2), 13 l., 18 r., 24, 25, 30/31, 32 (3), 58/59, 70 l., 84 r., 88 (bottom), 89 (bottom); Deutscher Fernseh-Dienst/defd 46, 60 (2), 61 (3), 83 bottom; dieKleinert/ Zimmermann 55; dpa 69 top r.; Florida State University 14/15; Lutz Hiller 2, 6, 7, 32/33, 37 r., 40/41, 50/51, 73 r., 84 l., 86/87, 96; Lutz Jahrmarkt 11 top l., 17, 35 r., 56 center, 65 center, 78 bottom, 79 top, 91 bottom l.; Kloster Andechs 76/77; Peer Kugler 21 (2); RASTAL 36–39 (11); Redaktionsbüro Pini 10, 11 top r., 16 l., 22 l., 35 l., 44 top, 48 bottom, 77 (top), 82 (4), 83 (7), 94; Stockfood 18/19, 40, 41, 52/53, 63, 85, 88 (top), 89 (2), 92/93; Ullstein 9 (top r.), 27, 90; Voller Ernst 8 (6), 9 (3), 40/41, 57, 69 r.

Special thanks for pictures and advice go to: Air France, Association of Brewers, USA, Balik Räucheri, Bayerische Staatsbrauerei Weihenstephan, Bayern Tourismus, Beck's/Interbrew, Beer Can Collectors of America, Belgien Tourismus, Mario Babilon, Brasseurs Gayant, Brauerei Altenmünster, Brauerei Aying, Brauerei Schloss Eggenberg, British Airways, Peter Broeker, Budweiser Budvar, Büttenpapierfabrik Gmund, DIE KOELNER, Einbecker Brauhaus, Erdinger Weißbräu, Fachverlag Hans Carl, Flensburger Brauerei, Fuller, Guhl, Heineken Deutschland, Hofbräuhaus, Holsten Brauerei, IBV, Kirin Europe, Märklin, Mulberry, Pilsner Urquell, PRevent, Radeberger Gruppe, Riedel Glas, Rogue Ale, Rugenbräu, Sister Doris Engelhard, Servicebüro Die Bayerischen Biere, Schussenrieder, signum[kom, Singha Deutschland, Skol, South African Brewers, Tuborg Deutschland, Unicer, unisono Markenkommunikation

The editor and publishers have made every effort during the production process to trace the owners of the rights to all other pictures. Individuals and organizations who may not have been contacted and to whom the rights to pictures used in this publication belong are asked to contact the publishers.